THE G.I. SERIES

U.S. Special Operations Forces in the Cold War

Rangers of the 1st Battalion, 75th Ranger in formation at Ft. Stewart, GA in October, 1977, with black beret, Ranger beret flash, Ranger distinctive insignia on the flash, and Ranger scroll. (U.S.A.)

THE G.I. SERIES

THE ILLUSTRATED HISTORY OF THE AMERICAN SOLDIER, HIS UNIFORM AND HIS EQUIPMENT

U.S. Special Operations Forces in the Cold War

Leroy Thompson

Greenhill Books
LONDON

Stackpole Books
PENNSYLVANIA

Greenhill Books

U.S. Special Operations Forces in the Cold War
first published 2002 by Greenhill Books, Lionel
Leventhal Limited,
Park House, 1 Russell Gardens, London NW11 9NN
www.greenhillbooks.com
and
Stackpole Books, 5067 Ritter Road, Mechanicsburg,
PA 17055, USA

British Library Cataloguing in Publication Data:

Thompson, Leroy
Special operations forces in the Cold War. – (The G.I.
series: the illustrated history of the American soldier,
his uniform and his equipment; v. 27)
1. Special Forces (Military science) – United States –
History   2. Cold War   3. United States – Armed
Forces – Uniforms 4. United States – Armed Forces –
Insignia 5. United States – Armed Forces – Equipment
I. Title
356.1'6'0973'09045

ISBN I-85367-506-7

Library of Congress Cataloging in Publication data
A catalog record is available.

Front cover illustration: Rangers of the 2nd Ranger
Battalion move out to secure a landing zone during a
drill. (Appears courtesy of the 2nd Ranger Bn)

Thanks are due to Ian Phillips, who provided
additional information for the captions.

Edited by Andy Oppenheimer
Designed by David Gibbons, DAG Publications Ltd
Layout by Anthony A. Evans, DAG Publications Ltd
Printed in China

CREDITS
U.S.A. = U.S. Army, U.S.A.F. = U.S. Air Force, U.S.N. =
U.S. Navy, U.S.M.C. = U.S. Marine Corps.

U.S. SPECIAL OPERATIONS FORCES IN THE COLD WAR

As the Cold War grew even chillier after the Korean conflict (1950–53), the United States put even more emphasis on highly trained special operations forces to operate behind enemy lines should the Cold War turn hot, to train potential guerrillas within the Communist bloc, and to operate against Communist guerrillas attempting to topple democratic governments. The Vietnam War (1959–1975) particularly engendered the rapid expansion of special operations forces who could operate in Viet Cong 'safe areas' and gather intelligence or deny safe havens to the guerrillas. In the post-Vietnam era many of these special operations forces would evolve into counter-terrorist forces or other highly trained specialists in low-intensity conflict.

In 1951, the Ranger units operating in Korea were deactivated and their personnel merged with other infantry or airborne units. Later in that same year, the Ranger Department was activated so that the skills of the Rangers would remain within the U.S. Army. However, rather than training Ranger formations, the Ranger Department was charged with training officers and NCOs in Ranger skills so that they could perform their missions with conventional infantry units more effectively.

Although Ranger units no longer existed as separate units, many commanders saw the need for elite light infantry units which could operate behind enemy lines, particularly for gathering timely tactical intelligence. As a result, in 1958, the first Long Range Reconnaissance Patrol (LRRP) units were formed in Germany. In 1966, a six-week (Long Range Patrol) LRP course was inaugurated at Ft. Benning. To teach the same skills to troops in Vietnam, the U.S. Army Special Forces also set up a three-week MACV (Military Assistance Command Vietnam) Recondo School at Nha Trang.

In 1967, LRP companies were formed in Vietnam and attached to each company and division. Operating in four-man patrols, these 'lurps' were used to gather intelligence, and for target acquisition for artillery or aircraft, raids, ambushes, and snatches of enemy troops for interrogation. In 1969, the LRP companies were given the lineage of Merrill's Marauders and assigned to the 75th Infantry Regiment, although each company remained assigned to an infantry division or corps. The year 1969 also saw the LRP companies designated Ranger companies, even though many of the personnel assigned had not graduated from the Ranger course. Many Ranger-qualified officers and NCOs did serve in Vietnam, including in LRP units, but approximately 2,000 Ranger Department graduates also served as advisors to the Vietnamese Rangers.

While the LRP/Ranger units in Vietnam were learning to operate in the jungle environment, a special LRP unit was formed at Ft. Richardson, Alaska. Designated the 'Arctic Rangers,' the members of this unit were trained not only for traditional LRP missions, but also for rescues in the Arctic, particularly in the case of airliners which could go down flying the polar route.

After the Vietnam War, most of the LRP units were disbanded. In fact, by 1973, only two LRP companies remained in the entire active U.S. Army. The appreciation of the need for tactical intelligence, however, inspired many divisional commanders to form provisional LRRP units within their commands during the early 1980s. Long Range Surveillance Companies were first activated in 1985.

The 1973 'Yom Kippur War' between Israel and neighboring Arab countries also motivated the Army to reform specialized Ranger units. The 1st Battalion/75th Rangers was formed in 1974 at Ft. Benning, Georgia. It should be noted that, unlike World War II Ranger battalions, the members of the 75th Rangers are airborne qualified as well as Ranger qualified. To offer a quickly deployable Ranger battalion on each coast of the U.S.A., the 2nd Battalion/75th Rangers was formed later in 1974 at Ft. Lewis, Washington. In 1978, the 1/75 Rangers were moved from Ft. Benning to Hunter Army Airfield, though the Ranger Department's training cadre remained at Ft. Benning. Then, in 1986, a third Ranger battalion, the 3/75th was formed. Trained for operations in urban, jungle, desert, mountain, cold weather, and amphibious environments, the Rangers are prepared to spearhead U.S. military operations anywhere in the world. One of their missions, in fact, is to parachute in and seize airfields so that other troops may be speedily air-landed in a troop buildup, a mission they performed during the U.S. operations on the island of Grenada.

The mission of the U.S. Army Special Forces continued to evolve during the Cold War. Although many ODAs (Operational Detachment A, the basic 12-man Special Forces operating unit) continued to train for potential missions in support of anti-Communist guerrillas in specific countries, the Special Forces' expertise in guerrilla warfare, combined with their language skills and knowledge of other cultures, made them the logical troops to serve in counter-insurgency warfare operations as well. As a result, John F. Kennedy, a great believer in Special Forces, not only authorized the wearing of the green beret but also ordered the expansion of Special Forces.

Without elaborating on various changes in designation, by the early 1960s the 1st Special Forces Group (SFG) (Airborne) had been formed with an orientation towards Asia, while the 10th Special Forces Group (Airborne) specialized in Europe. In 1961, the 5th Special Forces Group (Airborne) was formed for service in South-East Asia. Three other groups were formed in 1963 – the 3rd SFG (Abn) for Africa, the 6th SFG (Abn) for the Middle East, and the 8th SFG (Abn) for Latin America. Additionally, there were Special Forces Groups within the U.S. Army Reserve and National Guard.

The 12-man Operational Detachment A (ODA) was a very flexible formation which possessed an array of skills vital for guerrilla or counter-guerrilla warfare. Although designations have changed slightly during the years, the basic ODA has normally contained the following personnel:

- Detachment Commander (usually a captain)
- Executive Officer
- Operations Sergeant
- Assistant Operations Sergeant
- Heavy Weapons Leader
- Light Weapons Leader
- Medical Sergeant
- Medical Assistant
- Communications Supervisor
- Communications Operator
- Engineering Sergeant
- Engineer

Each team member is cross-trained in at least one other specialty, which allows an ODA to be divided in half to allow personnel to work with a greater number of guerrillas.

The Special Forces really achieved recognition through their commitment to the conflict in Vietnam. Teams from the Special Forces had been operating in Vietnam since 1957 when they began training Vietnamese special operations forces. The 77th SFG (Abn), which would later become the 7th SFG (Abn), also helped form and train the Vietnamese Rangers. By 1961, the Special Forces presence in Vietnam had increased substantially as teams trained indigenous irregulars, such as the Montagnards, in an attempt to counter Communist control of the countryside. By the mid-1960s, Special Forces fighting camps had been established in many of the contested areas to gather intelligence, provide a base for patrols, and to interdict Viet Cong supply routes. Special Forces would eventually train the Civilian Irregular Defense Forces as well as special reaction forces known as MIKE Forces.

To gather intelligence in Viet Cong controlled areas, various reconnaissance units were formed by Special Forces between 1964 and 1966, including Projects Delta, Sigma, Omega, and Gamma. The best known of special reconnaissance (recon) units, however, was MACV/SOG (Military Assistance Command Vietnam/Special Operations Group). MACV/SOG was not strictly a Special Forces operation as personnel from the SEALs (Sea, Air, and Land), Marine Corps Recon, and other units were also attached. SOG carried out various missions, including cross-border operations into Laos, Cambodia, and North Vietnam.

Special Forces were involved in various other special operations in Vietnam, including POW rescues – the best known of which was the 1970 Son Tay Raid into North Vietnam, involvement in the Phoenix Program to destroy the Viet Cong infrastructure, and rescues of downed pilots, among many others. Special Forces personnel also worked with Thai, Philippine, South Korean, Australian, and New Zealand special forces who were deployed to Vietnam.

As the U.S. commitment in Vietnam began to abate, some Special Forces Groups were deactivated, including the 3rd in 1969 and the 6th in 1971. The 5th and 7th SFGs (Abn) absorbed the missions in Africa and the Middle East in their place. Other deactivations included the 8th SFG (Abn) in 1972

and the 1st SFG (Abn) in 1974. Eventually, the 7th SFG (Abn) would take over the Latin American mission formerly carried out by the 8th SFG (Abn). In 1984, the 1st SFG (Abn) was reactivated for the Asian mission.

Special Forces were also assigned to counter-terrorist missions in 1978 with the formation of Special Forces Detachment 'Delta.' First used in the abortive Iranian hostage rescue mission, Delta was later used during the operations in Grenada and in various other clandestine missions.

Throughout the Cold War, the Special Forces have been U.S. military ambassadors to many Third World countries as they have helped train the airborne, commando, or special forces of those countries as well as taking part in many humanitarian missions following earthquakes, floods, or other disasters. As a result, they developed many relationships which would prove invaluable during a conflict in the area. Special Forces also continued to train for possible commitment to a major conflict against Communist forces should a war have started in Asia or Europe.

Although today's Marine Corps special operations forces owe some debt to the World War II Raiders, their real predecessors are the World War II Amphibious Scouts and the Korean War Reconnaissance Company. By 1955, the Marines had two divisional Recon Companies and two Force Recon companies as well as a reserve Recon Company. In 1957, the two Force Recon companies had a strength of 14 officers and 149 enlisted personnel. The next year saw the Divisional Recon Companies expanded to battalion strength of 29 officers and 491 enlisted personnel. Since the divisional recon personnel in particular performed a mission somewhat similar to the Army's Long Range Recon Patrols, many Recon Marines during this period attended Army Ranger training.

To clarify the missions of these recon units, it should be understood that a Recon Battalion is attached to each Marine Amphibious Force/Division. These battalions may be broken down to a platoon of one officer and 20 enlisted personnel for assignment to a Marine Amphibious Unit. For operations, the basic Marine Recon unit is a four-man team. Among the missions carried out by recon units are beach reconnaissance, mapping of terrain, and locating enemy positions. In addition to the Recon Battalion, there is also the Force Recon Company, which includes personnel trained as combat swimmers and parachutists as well as Recon Marines. The Force Recon Company will normally be used for deep reconnaissance prior to a landing.

All Recon Marines have attended the Basic Amphibious Reconnaissance Course, which includes patrolling, rappelling, boat insertions and extractions, communications, sketching, photography, and demolitions.

The largest commitment of Recon Marines came during the Vietnam War, when the 1st and 3rd Recon Battalions, as well as the 1st and 3rd Force Recon companies, served in the country. In addition to carrying out their normal reconnaissance functions, some Recon Marines served as advisors to Vietnamese Marines, as well as liaison with the South Korean Marine Brigade or with local hamlet defense forces. Marine Recons were also assigned to MACV/SOG. Since many Recons were trained as Scout/Snipers as well, they were also used to carry out missions to eliminate members of the Viet Cong infrastructure.

During the 1970s, as the recon mission expanded after the end of the Vietnam War, Arctic and desert warfare training also become critical elements of creating the Recon Marine. Because Marine Recons are often advance-deployed with Marine Amphibious Units, which have the mission of protecting American civilians anywhere in the world, Recons receive hostage rescue training and various other special operations training. The need for more highly trained Force Recon personnel resulted in the creation of an additional Force Recon Company in 1987.

Two other Marine Corps units that sometimes perform special operations missions normally contain a substantial number of Recon Marines. The Marine Fleet Anti-Terrorism Security Teams, which are charged with countering attacks on Naval or Marine Corps installations or ships, receive some special operations training, particularly related to building clearing, hostage rescue, and close combat. Members of the ANGLICO (Air and Naval Gunfire Liaison Company) have normally received parachute and combat swimmer training and are therefore frequently ex-Force Recon Marines. This unit has performed the mission of offering air and naval air gunfire support to U.S. Army airborne, Ranger, or other special operations personnel as well as allied forces who may need such support.

After Korea, the UDTs (Underwater Demolition Teams) continued to perform their missions as the Navy's beach recon and clearing units; however, during the early 1960s, John F. Kennedy, a great believer in special operations forces, ordered the Navy to develop its own special warfare capability. As a result, parachuting and small unit tactics were added to small-boat and SCUBA operations to form the SEAL Teams. Initially there were two teams, each with 10 officers and 50 enlisted men. SEAL Team I was assigned to Coronado, California, and SEAL Team II to Little Creek, Virginia. The practice of assigning odd-numbered SEAL Teams to the West Coast of the U.S.A. and even-numbered teams to the East Coast has continued until today. UDTs remained in existence along with the SEALs, each performing their own specialized missions, although in the early 1970s some UDTs were phased out. The last UDTs were converted to SEAL Teams in 1983.

The Vietnam War saw the first opportunity for the SEALs to put their combination of waterborne and land tactics to the test, and they passed with an 'A+.' In Vietnam, SEAL Team I and SEAL Team II were both deployed, especially in the MeKong Delta with its labyrinth of waterways. SEALs were assigned to carry out reconnaissance, carry out intelligence gathering raids, perform demolition missions (reportedly even in North Vietnam), set ambushes, carry out POW rescues, train Vietnamese combat swimmers (the LDNN*), and train the Provincial Recon Units (PRUs) who acted as the 'teeth' for the Phoenix Program.

As a result of the Vietnam experience, SEAL Team missions have evolved to include:

- raids to destroy enemy facilities or shipping on or near the water;
- infiltration or exfiltration of agents or guerrillas via the water, or rescue of U.S. civilian or military prisoners held near the water or on ships;
- reconnaissance and intelligence gathering missions;
- counter-insurgency or counter-guerrilla operations on or near the water;
- deception operations to simulate a landing and tie down enemy troops;
- foreign special operations troops training;
- counter-terrorist missions, including rescues or 'surgical eliminations.'

To carry out their missions, the SEALs primarily use closed-circuit SCUBA gear, which does not release bubbles that

*Lien Doc Nguoi Nhia: "soldiers who fight under the sea".

would locate the swimmer. SEALs also have various types of sophisticated boats and midget submarines. The SDV (swimmer delivery vehicle), a two-man midget submarine, has been widely used by the SEALs. To aid the SEALs in their missions, during the 1980s Special Boat Squadrons were formed, with SBR-1 on the West Coast and SBR-2 on the East Coast.

In 1980, the SEALs were given the additional mission of carrying out maritime counter-terrorist operations, with SEAL Team VI formed and trained for operations against ships, oil rigs, or shore installations where Americans might be held hostage or where counter-terrorist operations might be required.

Another mission which the SEALs absorbed during the post-Vietnam era was providing amphibious-ready platoons to accompany marine amphibious task forces and give them additional beach surveying, mine clearing, or other underwater capabilities. Although the Marine Recon troops assigned to marine amphibious units (MAUs) are trained for underwater operations, they do not receive the same level of such training as SEALs; therefore, the SEALs enhance the operational ability of these Marine units which are often termed 'America's 911,' since they are the first to respond when American citizens or interests are threatened.

In 1983, the SEALs took part in operations on Grenada. Their beach surveys prior to the Marine landings proved quite valuable, although some SEALs were lost at sea in another operation. Members of the SEALs who were sent to rescue British Governor-General Sir Paul Scoon on the island were also pinned down in his residence.

As the United States carried out maritime operations in the Persian Gulf, the SEALs also saw action in boarding ships and in raids against Iranian oil rigs, among other missions. By this time period, typical SEAL Team strength had reached 25 officers and 150 enlisted personnel. In addition to SEAL Team VI, three other teams also were formed during the 1980s. SEAL Team III was formed in 1983 and SEAL Teams IV and V were formed in 1984, primarily from former members of the UDT. To act as the command group for the SEAL Teams, Naval Special Warfare Group I was formed at Coronado and Naval Special Warfare Group II at Little Creek. In addition to the teams under each Group, there were also SEALs which came directly under group command.

Air Force special operations can trace its genesis to World War II supply missions for Merrill's Marauders or small plane operations in support of the OSS. However, modern Air Force SOF can on the whole trace their lineage most directly to the Air Commandos formed in 1961, as part of John F. Kennedy's emphasis on special operations forces. During the Vietnam War, the Air Commandos, who would be re-designated the 1st Special Operations Wing (SOW), in 1968, flew a variety of aircraft which allowed them to support special ops ground forces or conventional infantry. One of the most useful planes used by the Air Commandos was the A1E 'Skyraider,' a World War II prop-driven aircraft which could fly low and slow and carry an incredible array of ordnance. Air Force special ops squadrons would also fly the various fixed wing gunships which attacked traffic along the Ho Chi Minh Trail in support of 'Igloo White,' or carried out other special missions. The first of these gunships, the AC-47 'Puff the Magic Dragon,' was equipped with three 7.62-mm miniguns which could deliver withering fire as it circled overhead. Later gunships based on the AC-119 and the AC-130 carried even heavier armament.

In the post-Vietnam era, the Air Force retained the 1st Special Operations Wing, although many of the pilots for the special aircraft were drawn from the Air Force Reserve. In 1983, the 1st SOW was placed under the 2nd Air Division at Hulbert Field. Missions include support of unconventional warfare (including escape and evasion, guerrilla operations, sabotage, insertion or extraction of special operations forces, re-supply of special operations forces, psychological operations, and support of friendly forces).

By the 1980s, the 1st SOW was flying the following aircraft:

MC-130E 'Combat Talon,' an aircraft crammed with sophisticated electronics which allow terrain-hugging flying and precise delivery of troops or supplies;

MC-130E 'Spectre,' a gunship equipped with 2 x 20 mm Vulcan cannons, 1 x 40 mm Bofors cannon, and 1 x 105 mm howitzer;

MC-130E STAR (surface to air recovery) system, which allows two persons or 500 lbs of equipment to be plucked from the ground or water;

HH-53H PAVE LOW III Super Jolly Green Giant, a long-range, special operations helicopter designed to fly at night or in adverse weather conditions.

The 1st Special Operations Wing has continued to provide support for special operations, including drug interdiction operations in Latin America. The Air Force's combat control teams also fall under the 1st SOW. Combat control teams were developed to fill the need for integral Air Force airborne pathfinders once the Air Force became separate from the Army. Originally organized in 1953, the combat control teams have allowed the U.S. armed forces to have forward air control capability wherever they are deployed. Trained in airborne, scuba, and other insertion methods, the combat control teams can parachute in with the Rangers to seize an air base and establish an airhead or jump into an isolated Special Forces camps to bring in re-supply. Still another mission for the combat control teams could be a parachute insertion to call in air supply or air strikes in support of guerrillas allied with the U.S.A.

One Air Force unit which can be classified as a 'special operations' force deserves that designation primarily because of its intensive training and its operations behind enemy lines, more than its traditional combat role. Air Force Pararescuemen, known as the 'PJs' in Air Force jargon for parachute jumpers, have the mission of rescuing U.S. Air Force or other personnel who go down behind enemy lines. Although the PJs existed in a basic form during the Korean War, the unit was greatly expanded during the Vietnam War, in which it retrieved numerous pilots who had been shot down. The PJs also achieved a certain notoriety when in 1958 they were assigned the mission of retrieving U.S. astronauts and space capsules when they returned from missions to space.

The PJs are among the most highly trained personnel in the U.S. armed forces, being skilled in parachuting, SCUBA, mountain and arctic operations, survival, emergency medical techniques, and close combat tactics. Assigned to the Air Rescue and Recovery Service, the PJs operated very effectively from the HH-53 Jolly Green Giant and later from the Super Jolly Green Giant. In 1983, the Air Rescue and Recovery Service, along with other Air Force special operations units, came under the Military Airlift Command's 23rd Air Force. As of the mid-1980s there were only about 300 PJs worldwide.

Two other Air Force special operations units should be mentioned at least in passing. During the Vietnam War, attacks on U.S. air bases indicated that the traditional Air Force Security Police units, which provided base defense, were not armed or trained to face serious assaults. As a result, the U.S. Air Force Combat Security Police were formed and trained along the lines of the Army's Rangers. Three Combat Security Police squadrons – the 821st, 822nd, and 823rd – served in Vietnam between 1967 and 1971. Although disbanded after the Vietnam War, the Air Force has recently re-instituted a similar, highly trained ground combat unit. The Air Force also had throughout the Cold War a little known elite unit known as Combat Weather. Trained to parachute in and gather weather information about possible landing zones or areas upon which an air strike might be delivered, small Combat Weather teams reportedly operated in some extremely 'interesting' places during the Cold War.

Throughout the period between the Korean War and the dissolution of the Soviet Union, U.S. special operations forces had the mission of acting as force multipliers, intelligence gathering teams, counter-terrorist operators, and surgical raiding forces. The crumbling of the Soviet Union did not really change this mission, only its targets.

FOR FURTHER READING

Barker, Geoffrey T., *A Concise History of U.S. Army Special Operations Forces with Lineage and Insignia.* Fayetteville, NC: Anglo-American Publishing Company, 1988.

Buford, John, *LRRPs in Action.* 'Combat Troops #11.' Carrollton, TX: Squadron Signal Publications, 1994.

Collins, John M., *Green Berets, SEALs, and Spetsnaz: U.S. and Soviet Special Military Operations.* Washington: Pergamon-Brassey's, 1987.

The Green Berets. 'Gung-Ho Magazine Special,' 1983.

Halburton, Hans, *Green Berets: Unconventional Warriors.* Novato, CA: Presidio Press, 1988.

Harclerode, Peter (ed.), *The Elite and Their Support.* 'Vol I'. Hartley Whitney: Strategic Publishing Ltd, no date.

Katz, Samuel M., *Today's Green Berets: The U.S. Army's Special Forces Groups (Airborne).* (Hong Kong): Concord Publications, 1996.

Katz, Samuel M., *U.S. Navy SEALs: America's Toughest Commandos.* Hong Kong: Concord Publications, 1993.

Melson, Charles D., *Marine Recon, 1940–1990.* 'Osprey Elite Series'. London: Osprey Publishing, 1994.

Pararescue 'Iron Men of the Air Force.' Gung-Ho Magazine Special, 1987.

'Ranger.' Gung-Ho Magazine Special, 1984.

'Recon/Force Recon: The Marine Corps Elite Unit.' Gung-Ho Magazine Special, 1985.

Rottman, Gordon L., *U.S. Army Ranger and LRRP unit, 1942–1987.* 'Osprey Elite Series,' London: Osprey Publishing, 1987.

Rottman, Gordon L., *U.S. Army Special Forces, 1952–1984.* 'Osprey Elite Series,' London: Osprey Publishing, 1985.

Stanton, Shelby, *Rangers at War: Combat Recon in Vietnam.* New York: Orion Books, 1992.

Stubblefield, Gary and Hans Halberstadt, *Inside the U.S. Navy SEALs.* Osceola, WI: Motorbooks International, 1995.

Thompson, Leroy, *De Oppresso Liber: The Illustrated History of the U.S. Army Special Forces.* Boulder, CO: Paladin Press, 1987.

Thompson, Leroy, *Uniforms of the Elite Forces.* Poole: Blandford Press, 1982.

Thompson, Leroy. *U.S. Elite Forces – Vietnam.* 'Combat Troops #7,' Carrollton, TX: Squadron-Signal Publications, 1985.

'U.S. Navy SEALs.' Gung-Ho Magazine Special, 1985.

Above: U.S. Army Rangers of the 2nd Ranger Battalion practice building clearing operations at Ft. Lewis, WA, during the 1980s; some of the Rangers are armed with Heckler & Koch MP5D suppressed sub-machineguns. (2nd Ranger Bn)

Right: Members of the 7th SFG (Abn) give ground training as part of parachute qualification for Latin American trainees. (U.S.A.)

Left: Members of the 7th SFG (Abn) give ranger training to troops in El Salvador during 1974. (U.S.A.)

Below: Special Forces personnel train with field amplification equipment used for 'psy ops' in counter-insurgency operations. (U.S.A.)

Right: Special Forces personnel must be prepared to give instruction on all types of weapons, including mortars. (U.S.A.)

Right: Members of the Special Forces give parachute instruction using the MC1-1 parachute in El Salvador. (U.S.A.)

Below: Special Forces trained irregulars patrol the MeKong Delta using an air boat. (U.S.A.)

Above left: Member of the 5th SFG (Abn) with indigenous troops in Vietnam; the colors of the Vietnamese flag are on the 5th SFG (Abn) beret flash. (U.S.A.)

Above: Special Forces advisor with irregular troops in Vietnam. He is wearing the same tiger stripes as his troops. (Dring)

Left: During jungle warfare training in Panama, a member of the 7th SFG (Abn) acts as a Buddhist priest being interrogated by a member of the 82nd Airborne Division. (U.S.A.)

Right: Special Forces trained and led irregulars on patrol in Vietnam. (Dring)

Right: Women soldiers assigned to the 7th SFG (Abn) receive field survival training at Ft. Bragg during 1976. (U.S.A.)

Right: Member of the Special Forces practices preparing a branch for building a shelter or booby trap; note the subdued SF insignia and SF and Airborne tabs. The knife being used is a Parrish hollow-handled survival knife. This knife was very popular with Special Forces personnel since escape and evasion items could be carried in the hollow handle. (Parrish)

Left: SEALs during an attack on Viet Cong bunkers in the MeKong Delta. (U.S.N.)

Left: SEALs wading ashore for operations in the MeKong Delta. (U.S.N.)

Left: U.S.A.F. Combat Controller brings in a transport aircraft at a base in Vietnam. (U.S.A.F.)

Right: U.S. Marine Recons practicing their use of cover for intelligence gathering operations. (U.S.M.C.)

Right: An Air Force PJ checks the jungle penetrator aboard his helicopter. Note that his maroon beret is tucked into the cargo pocket of his flight suit. He is wearing parachutist's wings on the left breast of his M-1A flight jacket. (U.S.A.F.)

Below: U.S. Ranger instructor shows the proper technique for catching, cooking, and eating snakes during ranger training. The Ranger tab can be seen over the beret flash. (U.S.A.)

Left: A minigunner aboard an Air Rescue and Recovery Service HH-53 prepares to give covering fire to PJs on a rescue mission. (U.S.A.F.)

Below: Members of a U.S.A.F Combat Security Police unit do a sweep of an air base to check for infiltrators. (U.S.A.F.)

Above: Maj. Gen. Ned Moore visits members of the Long Range Patrol 'Arctic Fox' in Alaska during 1962. This was an LRP unit specially trained for cold weather operations. It appears that Gen. Moore is wearing the Colt General Officers pistol on his belt, while the members of 'Arctic Fox' wear OD 108 wool/nylon field shirts, featuring the 'polar bear' patch of the Alaskan Command. The men also wear OD field trouser shells over their regular woolen trousers, which provide additional insulation in the cold climate. (U.S.A.)

Below: Members of LRP 'Arctic Fox' in Alaska, July, 1962. Among this unit's missions were operations against potential Soviet Spetsnaz along the Alaskan coast. (U.S.A.)

Opposite page, top: Members of Company C, Long Range Patrol, 58th Infantry Division on a march in Holland during July, 1967. This is a particularly good view of the mountain rucksacks issued to these troops by the US Army. This unit was assigned long range recon missions for U.S. forces assigned to NATO. (U.S.A.)

Opposite page, bottom: A U.S. Advisor to the Vietnamese Rangers watches hand-to-hand combat training. Note that the U.S. advisor wears the red BDQ (Biet Dong Quan) beret with Ranger badge and the BDQ pocket badge. The beret is peaked in BDQ Style. Also at this time, U.S. troops were still allowed to carry personally owned handguns, in this case a revolver. His 'Western-style' pistol belt is also non-issue and likely to be privately acquired. On the advisor's left hip he carries a Randall knife. (Society of Vietnamese Rangers)

Above: A U.S. Ranger advisor at the Duc My Ranger Training Center examines the leg of an instructor bandaged by a Ranger trainee. The trainees are using available camouflage materials. The U.S. captain carries an M2 carbine, the fully automatic version of the popular M1. (U.S.A.)

Above: During September, 1965, a U.S. SFC and an Australian warrant officer observe Vietnamese Ranger trainees coming down the 'death slide' at the Duc My Ranger Training Center. The U.S. sergeant wears the first-pattern jungle uniform, identifiable by its exposed buttons and shoulder straps. The uniform bears MACV (Military Assistance Command Vietnam) shoulder sleeve insignia. (U.S.A.)

Opposite page, top: U.S. Ranger advisors observes a Vietnamese Ranger searching a VC suspect. The Ranger holds an M1 Carbine fitted with its M4 bayonet. He appears to be equipped with locally-made pouches for magazines as opposed to the regular US-made items. The U.S. advisors wear the Vietnamese Ranger beret along with U.S. MACV SSI and 'Ranger' tab. (U.S.A.)

Opposite page, bottom: A LRRP from Company D (Ranger), 75th Infantry attached to the II Field Force acts as the point man for his team during May, 1970. (U.S.A.)

Opposite page: During a demonstration in March 1969 at the MACV Recondo School, an instructor explains the equipment worn by a LRRP (pronounced 'lurp'). The instructor wears the pocket patch of the MACV Recondo School. The LRRP wears tiger stripe camouflage utilities and boonie cap, and carries a camouflaged M-16 rifle. Note the combination of fragmentation and smoke grenades. (U.S.A.)

Right: A LRRP with the detonator for a Claymore mine in one hand and an M79 'Thumper' grenade launcher in the other. (U.S.A.)

Right: This LRRP wears the black beret occasionally encountered among some LRRP units with a locally made LRRP beret flash. The LRRP arc is worn over the 9th Infantry Division SSI. The subdued 9th Division 'Recondo' pocket patch is probably a locally procured item. The radio is a URC-10 used for emergency extraction or when other communications equipment has failed. (U.S.A.)

Left: Trainee at the MACV Recondo School practices helicopter insertions. (U.S.A.)

Right: Special Forces 1st Lt. undergoing training at Eglin Air Force Base during 1962. There is no beret flash behind the Lt's rank insignia. (U.S.A.)

Opposite page: Demonstration of rapelling at the Ranger Training Center at Ft. Benning, GA. The famous parachute jump towers in the background are a relic of World War II, and were erected for members of the embryonic U.S.A.F. who trained there. (U.S.A.)

Above: This advisor to the Vietnamese Rangers prepares to demonstrate how the Rangers got their nickname 'Snake Eaters.' (U.S.A.)

Opposite page: A member of the 75th Rangers, with equipment bag, just after landing during a practice parachute jump. (U.S.A.)

Above: Rangers parachuted into Grenada to seize an airfield as part of the operation to rescue U.S. medical students on the island. (U.S.A.)

Right: Members of the 77th SFG (Abn) practice field butchery in Colorado during 1955. (U.S.A.)

Below: Three parachutists from the 77th SFG (Abn) prepare to enter a sport parachute competition in April, 1958. Note that they are wearing the Special Forces arrowhead patch and 'Special Forces' tab. Their highly-polished 'Corcoran-style' jump boots were a cherished symbol of the SF paratrooper's elite status. (U.S.A.)

Opposite page: This captain of the 1st SFG (Abn), at Clark AFB in the Philippines in 1961, wears the green beret but with parachute oval and parachute wings rather than the flash which would be worn later. His utility shirt is early-pattern, cotton-sateen with an added pen pocket on the sleeve. He also wears a pistol belt characteristic of the World War II era. (U.S.A.)

Above: During 1962, troops from the 7th SFG (Abn) practice guerrilla warfare techniques in the mountains of West Virginia. The standard firearm for these troops is still the World War II issue M1 Garand rifle. The soldier in the right foreground is wearing the recently adopted red flash of the 7th SFG (Abn). (U.S.A.)

Opposite page, bottom: Members of the 7th SFG (Abn) practice patrolling tropical swamp land at Eglin AFB during June, 1962. The green beret was in general wear at this time. The full-color insignia worn by these troops is clearly visible in this verdant landscape. Experiences in Vietnam led directly to the introduction of the black/green 'subdued' insignia for better concealment. (U.S.A.)

Above: A sergeant of the 7th SFG (Abn) stands guard as his team practices a jungle insertion from a small boat during 1962. He carries the M1 Garand rifle and wears a green beret with 7th SFG (Abn) flash. He also wears the Special Forces arrowhead and tab. (U.S.A.)

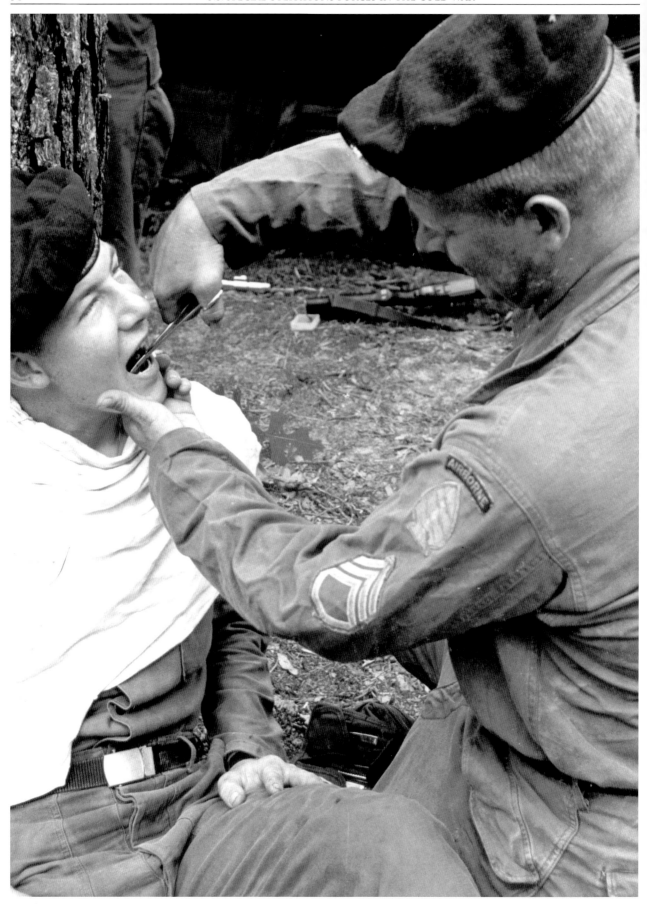

Above: During September, 1962, members of the 7th SFG (Abn) participate in a guerrilla warfare exercise in the Nantahala National Forest in North Carolina. Special Forces were trained in rugged areas similar to the kind they would encounter while working with guerrillas in Europe or Latin America. (U.S.A.)

Opposite page: Special Forces medics, such as this one from the 7th SFG (Abn), are trained to carry out dental care, including pulling teeth. The patient wears a black web trouser belt with brass roller buckle – later belts had a blackened-brass buckle. (U.S.A.)

Right: This sergeant assigned to the 5th SFG (Abn) in Vietnam during December 1962 runs a commo check of his radio equipment. At this early date the 5th SFG (ABN) flash does not yet contain the colors of the Vietnamese flag as it would later. (U.S.A.)

Above: Members of the 7th SFG (Abn) at the John F. Kennedy Special Warfare School at Ft. Bragg in November, 1964. As with all Army personnel assigned to airborne units, these Special Forces soldiers wear their trousers bloused into their jump boots. (U.S.A.)

Opposite page, top: The Ton Le Chon Special Forces fighting camp viewed from the air. Note the mortar pits, artillery emplacements, and machinegun positions. The Special

Forces team would normally be based within the inner defenses. (author's collection)

Opposite page, bottom: A member of the 5th SFG (Abn) in Vietnam is presented the Silver Star for gallantry. He wears parachute wings and a Combat Infantryman's badge on his left breast and Vietnamese parachute wings on his right breast. This is another example of the early-pattern jungle uniform, with its exposed buttons and shoulder straps. (U.S.A.)

Opposite page, top: Aerial view of the Thien Ngon Special Forces fighting camp; this camp uses the star design reminiscent of Renaissance fortresses designed by Vauban. (author's collection)

Opposite page, bottom: A Special Forces heavy weapons leader supervises CIDG (Civilian Irregular Defense Group) indigenous troops as they prepare to fire a 105-mm howitzer. The indigenous soldiers wear a 'Tiger Stripe' camouflage uniform, popular in-country and one of many recorded variants. (U.S.A.)

Above: An American Special Forces commander of a MIKE Force composed of Chinese Nungs. On his tiger stripes he wears 'Airborne' and 'Ranger' tabs over his MIKE Force shoulder sleeve insignia. (U.S.A.)

Above: Members of Mobile Launch Team One assigned to MACV/SOG at Phu Ba in 1970. Their STABO extraction harnesses enabled the troops to be extracted by helicopter while leaving their hands free to fire at the enemy or perform other tasks. (Society of Vietnamese Rangers)

Opposite page, top: Experimental jungle boots designed for use by recon teams of MACV/SOG so that soldiers would not leave distinctive boot prints on jungle trails. (EAGLE Magazine)

Opposite page, bottom: Members of the U.S. Special Forces practice movement down a trail. Note that the point man wears the Special Forces distinctive insignia on his beret flash and carries an Uzi sub-machinegun. The third soldier is armed with an AK-47. Special Forces members receive extensive training with foreign weapons. (U.S.A.)

Left: Members of some Special Forces-trained recon teams wore Viet Cong style black pajamas such as these, so that their profile would not immediately give them away along a trail. (West Point Museum)

Opposite page, top: Members of Special Forces practice movement down a stream bed to make it harder to pick up their trail. (U.S.A.)

Opposite page, bottom: A member of Special Forces prepares to practice his silent killing techniques during training. (U.S.A.)

Above: While a Special Forces communications specialist sets up his radio, other members of his unit set up a security perimeter. The soldier at the right carries a rope for crossing chasms or ascending or descending. (U.S.A.)

Opposite page: Special Forces train with many foreign special operations forces, such as this member of the Jordanian Special Forces. He wears U.S. parachute wings on his left breast – the single star indicates that he is of senior rank. (Adrian Bohlen)

Right: Many former members of Special Forces serve with the Central Intelligence Agency (CIA) training indigenous troops where official U.S. government involvement is not desirable. In some cases, Special Forces members are temporarily assigned to the CIA for training missions. One group of guerrillas trained by 'ex' members of the Special Forces were the anti-Sandinista 'Contras' in Nicaragua. This Contra uses the AK-47. (author's collection)

Opposite page, top: This group of Contra rebels is a typical guerrilla band of the type Special Forces is trained to support. (author's collection)

Opposite page, bottom: Note that, in addition to the M1 Carbine, at least one member of this Contra band is armed with a crossbow. Special Forces must be prepared to train 'indigs' with all types of weapons. This crossbowman may have been charged with silently killing enemy soldiers. (author's collection)

Above: To avoid odors which would give them away to the Viet Cong, SEALs normally did not bathe or shave prior to an insertion, hence this individual's unkempt appearance! (U.S.N.)

Opposite page, top: SEALs returning to base after a patrol in Operation Crimson Tide during September, 1967. The ration can is attached to the M-60 machineguns to help insure reliable feeding. (U.S.N.)

Opposite page, bottom: SEALs along with indigenous troops in Vietnam. Two SEALs on the left and the SEAL on the right carry the Stoner light machine guns favored by the SEALs. The special grenadier vest is worn by the SEAL standing second from right to carry 40-mm grenades. (U.S.N.)

Right: SEALs on a Mike Boat retire after destroying a Viet Cong fortification on the Bassac River in operations in Vietnam during September, 1967. (U.S.N.)

Opposite page: This SEAL in Vietnam wears tiger-stripe camouflage and a dive watch in addition to his gas mask. CS or other gas was often used to flush the Viet Cong from underground complexes. (U.S.N.)

Above: This SEAL carries the M-16 with the early XM148 40-mm grenade launcher mounted. The SEALs were one of the first units equipped with this predecessor to the M-203 grenade launcher. (U.S.N.)

Opposite page: SEAL wearing the camouflage beret sometimes encountered with members of the SEAL Teams in Vietnam; the scarf is actually cut from a piece of camouflaged parachute silk. (U.S.N.)

Right: SEALs being inserted from a Boston Whaler for a mission in the Rung Sat Special Zone in Vietnam during April, 1968. (U.S.N.)

Below: In October, 1968, SEALs man their weapons as they approach the shore in a PBR (Patrol Boat, River). (U.S.N.)

Above: A member of Seal Team One, climbs aboard a small craft of the Mobile Riverine Force. (U.S.N.)

Right: U.S. Marine Recon in scuba gear; Recon Marines are trained to infiltrate the beach under water. (U.S.M.C.)

Left: Marine Recon chuted up for a parachute insertion. Normally, Force Recon personnel are more likely to be used for parachute operations. This individual is wearing the paratrooper version of the M1-C helmet, identifiable by the 'Y' straps of its liner, and the web chin-cup. (U.S.M.C.)

Above: A Force Recon Marine in jungle utilities during a training mission at Camp Pendleton, California, during August, 1974. (U.S.M.C.)

Above: Recon Marines practicing helicopter operations at Camp Pendleton, CA, during 1970. The Marine in the foreground carries the M-14 rifle. (U.S.M.C.)

Opposite page, top: Marine Recons practicing insertion by inflatable boat. (U.S.M.C.)

Opposite page, bottom: During February 1974 members of the U.S.M.C. 1st Recon Battalion on a landing zone they have cleared for members of the 2nd Battalion, 5th Marines. There is a T-122 type angle-headed flashlight attached to the far-left trooper's suspenders. This design dates back to World War II, when it was supplied with various colored lenses for signalling purposes. (U.S.M.C.)

Opposite page, top: Recon Marines blend with their surroundings during a training exercise. (U.S.M.C.)

Opposite page, bottom: A member of the 1st Force Recon Company practices underwater operations. (U.S.M.C.)

Above: U.S. Marine Recons practice intelligence gathering. The Marine on the right carries an M3 'Grease Gun' and both wear camouflage head coverings fabricated from helmet covers. (U.S.M.C.)

Opposite page, top: Member of the 1st Recon Battalion practices repelling from a helicopter at Camp Pendleton during a demonstration on Armed Forces Day. (U.S.M.C.)

Opposite page, bottom: Members of Marine ANGLICO Teams such as this one possess many of the same skills as Recon

marines and are often drawn from those with Recon training. (U.S.M.C.)

Above: This U.S. Marine advisor is working with the local police chief and local defense force members in Vietnam tracking Viet Cong. (U.S.M.C.)

Opposite page, top: Marine advisors in Vietnam often had to perform training and liaison functions similar to those of the U.S. Special Forces. This U.S. Marine advisor is working with Vietnamese Marines on small boat operations. (U.S.M.C.)

Opposite page, bottom: From Vietnam to the present, the AC-130 gunship, the 'Spectre,' has remained an important weapon within the U.S. Air Force special operations arsenal. The installed M163 Vulcan rotary canons are capable of delivering a formidable volley of fire onto their targets. (U.S.A.F.)

Above: Marine advisors worked with 'Ruff Puffs' (Regional Forces, Popular Forces) in some areas, performing the same missions as undertaken by Special Forces advisors in other locations. Various elements of World War II weaponry are visible. There is an M1A1 airborne version of the M1 carbine (far left), an M3 SMG (right), and a 60-mm mortar (foreground). The compact M1A1 was suited to ARVN (Army of the Republic of Vietnam) forces, as it generally suited their smaller stature, as opposed to larger, full-powered rifles which might otherwise have been issued. (U.S.M.C.)

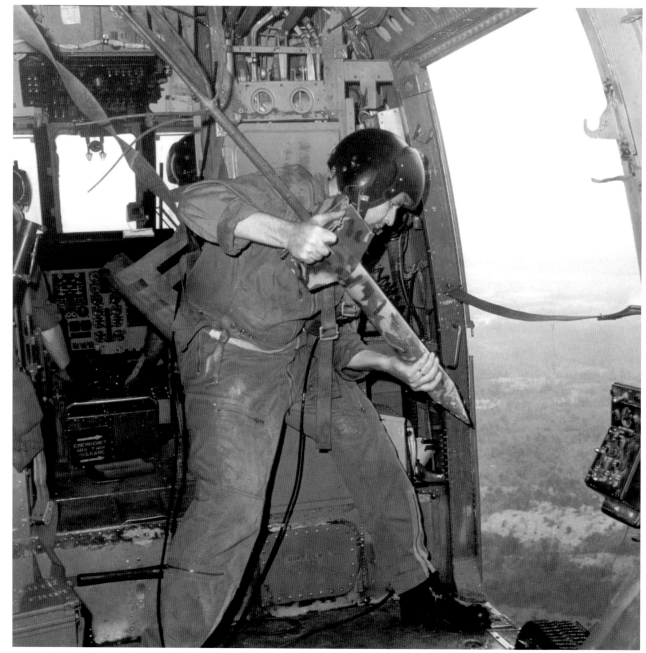

Opposite page top:
The forerunner to the
AC-130 gunship used
in Vietnam was the
AC-47 'Puff the Magic
Dragon.' (U.S.A.F.)

**Opposite page
bottom:** U.S.A.F.
special operations
personnel in Vietnam
were involved in
placing sensors, such
as this ADSID (air-
delivered seismic
sensor), along the Ho
Chi Minh Trail.
(U.S.A.F.)

Right: Members of a
U.S.A.F. Combat
Control Team (CCT)
wear the dark blue
beret with parachute
wings worn by CCTs.
(U.S.A.F.)

Below: A U.S.A.F. CCT
practices rope
techniques; note that
he wears a camouflage
boonie hat and carries
the short "CAR-15"
version of the M-16
rifle.

Opposite page:
Members of an Air
Force Combat Control
Team leave a
helicopter via a
'Trooper Ladder.'
(U.S.A.F.)

Right: Air Force
Pararescue personnel
winch a rescued
airman aboard their
helicopter. (U.S.A.F.)

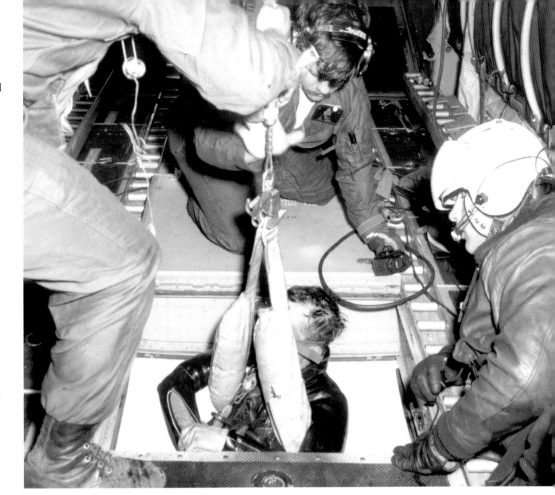

Below: An Air Force
Pararescueman
receives the Air Force
Cross for gallantry
during the Vietnam
War. The PJ receiving
the medal wears
senior parachute
wings. (U.S.A.F.)

Opposite page: An Air Force PJ descends on a jungle/forest penetrator from an HH-53 helicopter during training at Eglin AFB in May, 1968. He is wearing an unofficial 'duck-hunter' camouflage suit together with the ever-popular jungle boots. (U.S.A.F.)

Above: An Air Force PJ dons his scuba gear during a rehearsal for the recovery of an Apollo Space Capsule in 1968. (U.S.A.F.)

Above: An Air Rescue and Recovery Service HH-53 Super Jolly Green Giant being aerially refueled. These choppers have been used on many occasions by PJs to carry out rescue behind enemy lines. (U.S.A.F.)

Below: U.S.A.F. Combat Security Policemen training on an M2 .50-caliber machinegun at Phan Rang in Vietnam. They wear camouflage utilities, unlike most Air Force personnel. (U.S.A.F.)